What Does a Level Do?

by Robin Nelson

first step nonfiction

Lerner Publications Company · Minneapolis

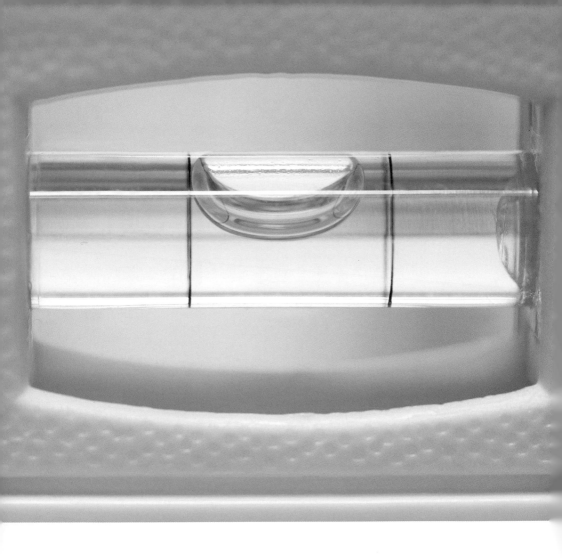

What tool is this?

It is a **level**.

Tools help us do jobs.

Levels make jobs easier.

Levels show if something is flat.

Levels work across and up and down.

A level has two flat bars.

Between the bars are small windows.

Inside each window is a **tube**.

A bubble moves in each tube.

Put the level on a shelf.

The bubble moves to the
center of the tube.

If the bubble is **centered**, the shelf is straight, or **even**.

If the bubble is not centered,
the shelf is not straight.

Builders use levels to build houses.

What can you do with a
level?

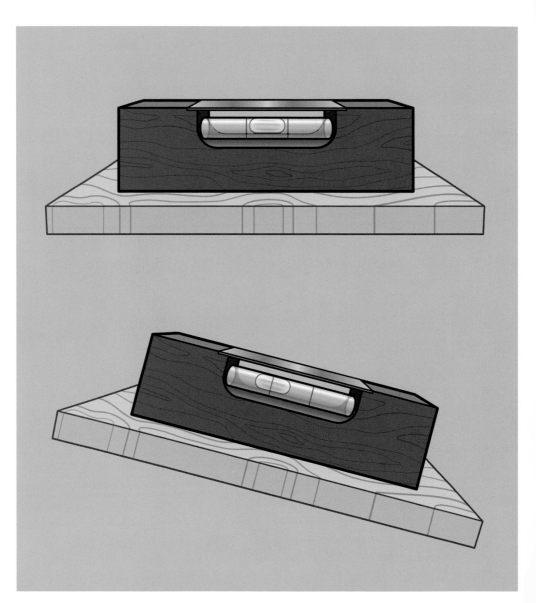

Why Do We Need Levels?

Why does a shelf have to be straight? What would happen if a shelf was not straight? If you do not use a level, the shelf might not fit together. Books on the shelf would slide down or fall over. A level helps you make sure your shelf is flat.

Safety First

 Ask a grown-up to help before using any tools.

 Wear safety glasses to protect your eyes.

 Roll up your sleeves. Tuck in your shirt. Tie back your hair. Take off any jewelry that might get in the way.

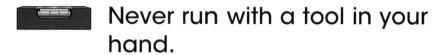 Never run with a tool in your hand.

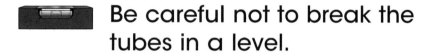 Be careful not to break the tubes in a level.

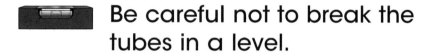 Put away the level when you are done with your job.

Glossary

 centered – in the middle

 even – flat and straight

 level – a tool used to see if something is flat

 tube – a long, round shape that holds liquid

Index

The images in this book are used with the permission of: © iStockphoto.com/parema, p. 2; © Ange/Alamy, pp. 3, 22; © iStockphoto.com/Frank van den Bergh, p. 4; © Heath Korvola/UpperCut Images/Getty Images, p. 5; © Assembly/Taxi/Getty Images, p. 6; © iStockphoto.com/Justin Horrocks, p. 7; © Rosli Othman/Shutterstock.com, pp. 8, 22; © iStockphoto.com/Mark Coffey, p. 9; © J. Helgason/Shutterstock.com, pp. 10, 22; © Todd Strand/Independent Picture Service, pp. 11, 13, 14, 15, 22; © Medioimages/Photodisc/Getty Images, p. 12; © Moodboard/123RF, p. 16; © Image Source/Getty Images, p. 17; © Laura Westlund/Independent Picture Service, pp. 18, 20, 21.

Front cover: © Glowimages/Getty Images.

Main body text set in ITC Avant Garde Gothic Std Medium 21/25.
Typeface provided by Adobe Systems.

Lerner Publications Company
A division of Lerner Publishing Group, Inc.
241 First Avenue North
Minneapolis, MN 55401 U.S.A.

Website address: www.lernerbooks.com

Library of Congress Cataloging-in-Publication Data

Nelson, Robin, 1971–
    What does a level do? / by Robin Nelson.
       p.   cm. — (First step nonfiction—tools at work)
    Includes index.
    ISBN 978–0–7613–8981–1 (lib. bdg. : alk. paper)
    1. Leveling—Juvenile literature. 2. Tools—Juvenile literature. I. Title.
TA607.N45 2013
526.3'6—dc23   2011039074

Manufactured in the United States of America
1 – BC – 7/15/12